12

The Apple, Doesn't Fall Far

School: Real Stories,
Real Parents,
Real Life

STEPHEN HAWN
MALA KRAL

Kos —
Thank you for all
you do to make
school. Mala
amazing.

Dedication

Jes, Rowan, Kaden and those on the way - Always My Inspiration

STEVE

To my Mom and Tutu to many - Thank you for teaching me:
the joy of play, the difference between right and wrong, the
firm foundation of faith, and living proof that love wins.

MALA

TABLE OF CONTENTS

Preface

"Summer 1974.
I'm 9 years old. By 7:30 a.m.,
I'm up and out of the house, or if it's
Saturday I'm up and doing
exactly what my father,
Big Jerry, has told me to do.
Might be raking, mowing,
digging holes or washing cars.

Summer 2016.
I'm tiptoeing out of the house,
on my way
to work, in an effort not to wake
my children who will undoubtedly
sleep until 11 am.
They may complete a couple of the chores
I've left in a list on the kitchen counter
for them, or they may eat stale Cheez-its
that were left in their
rooms 3 days ago,
in order to avoid the kitchen at all costs
and "not see the list."

USED WITH PERMISSION: RHONDA STEPHENS

The times have definitely changed. Some argue parents are getting the short end of the stick these days, while others claim kids are now being deprived of important life lessons. Through it all, middle school perseveres like a long-running soap opera. The characters may come and go and a million and one events may take place over the course of a week, but, through all the change and chaos, you can pick up right where you left off. After reading the heartwarming, heartbreaking, you gotta be kidding me, all too true and real stories in this book, you decide who is getting the short end of the stick.

Strange But True

"The surprising thing about young fools is how many survive to become old fools."

DOUG LARSON

Punish Me

During a Frisbee golf lesson in class, a student accidently threw a Frisbee into a tree. He immediately freaked out thinking he would get in trouble. His classmates and teachers tried to tell him not to worry about it, and that the wind would save it eventually. "Don't be so hard on yourself," they said. The student perseverated, repeatedly stating he had to be punished. The class said, "No. You don't need to be punished for this accident." As his volume increased, more and more students gathered around. This time the student tensed his body, closed his eyes, and insisted the teacher kick him in the privates as hard as he could.

Fattest Man

As a brand new, young teacher looking for my first real job, I went on my first interview for a job at a middle school teaching math and P.E. Feeling so excited about this opportunity, I prepared, overprepared, and practiced responses to anticipated questions. I focused on fitness, movement, and activity level…my philosophy for a healthy lifestyle. I arrived for my interview, was greeted by the office secretary (yep, that's what they were called back then), and patiently waited for the principal to meet with me…all the while, rehearsing my fitness protocol so I could impress the principal. After a brief wait, the office secretary ushered me back to the principal's office where I was greeted by truly the fattest man I had ever seen. I knew he would not be impressed by my fitness and movement philosophy. In fact, he might be embarrassed, angered, or mortified by it. My mind went blank. To this day, I have no idea what I said in that interview, but, I got the job.

Moist Palms

10/8/03

Please excuse Courtney ▮▮▮▮ from doing monkey bars, pull-up bar, & climbing the pole. She has a problem with moisture on the palms of her hands? (which makes her slip right off. I have the same problem—in fact I had to be excused from the same thing when I was at ▮▮▮▮. Maybe you can replace it with another activity. If you have any questions feel free to call. ▮▮▮▮

—Thank You,

▮▮▮▮

Bugs a Bubbling

It was just another day in the overcrowded locker room when crazy screeching sounds were echoing into the teachers' office. A concerned teacher ran into the locker room to see what was causing the disturbance. As the girls were screaming wildly and jumping up onto the locker room benches, a path was cleared so the teacher could see the source of the disturbance. Much to the amazement of the adolescent onlookers, and the experienced teacher for that matter, water was backing up out of the floor drains and live bugs came bubbling up by the thousands. As the teacher tried in vain to settle the students down, kids were jumping and running, all the while trying to get their P.E. clothes on in order to exit the locker room, to escape the moving floor of creepy bugs.

Sight, Sounds, Scents, and Snakes

Another regular day in the heavily occupied locker room when the screeching sounds were heard again. From the teachers' office, she could see the students jumping up on the benches, pointing and yelling at something on the ground. The teacher ran out anticipating, from past experience, bugs bubbling up from the drains. Instead, what the veteran teacher saw was even more gruesome. It was murky water and shards of toilet paper. The teacher shouted for the kids to exit the building and called the office reporting there was a plumbing emergency that needed immediate attention. The teacher insisted it was a major plumbing problem and the school would need outside help (i.e. a professional plumber as opposed to the trusty, overworked, site custodian) to resolve it. Once the building was cleared, a similar story emerged from the boys Physical Education side, and everyone knew there was a major problem. At the end of the period, a plumber working just outside the locker rooms and within the students' and staff members' sight, sound, and olfactory range removed the sewer line cover. Raw sewage flowed over the classroom as more screeching ensued. Then the plumber, super calm, whipped out a snake the size of a boa constrictor, to try to clear the drain. He successfully dislodged then pulled out the culprit, which was a pair of P.E. shorts! Photo below....go ahead, you know you wanna see it

Pogo-Stick Play

[redacted] played hard all evening on her pogo-stick. Her legs are very *tight* & *sore* this morning. Are you willing to modify her workout today?

[redacted] Cox [redacted] ·25·09

Flaming Hot Cheetos

No matter how any times the students are told NOT to eat in the locker room, they still do. It seems a dank and dark sweaty enclosed room is an appealing place for adolescents to munch on their favorite snack foods. We repeatedly remind them that snacking in the locker room attracts ants and cockroaches and rodents, not to mention it's gross, but students still insist on eating in there. On any given day, snack remnants including chips, crackers, pretzels, and Flaming Hot Cheetos (a middle school favorite) can be found strewn across the locker room floor. Mysteriously, the Flaming Hot Cheetos would disappear but all other snacks remained on the ground. Turns out Flaming Hot Cheetos are not just a favorite for middle schoolers…the resident rat loves them as well. During an entire academic year, every time someone left Flaming Hot Cheetos on the floor, the resident rat would carefully pick through the food options, selecting only the Flaming Hot Cheetos to munch. This was discovered one day after school, as a teacher was quietly working at her computer. She decided to investigate the strange "crunch, crunch, crunch" sounds she heard regularly in the locker room. And there he was, resident rat happily chomping away on the Flaming Hot Cheetos. This became a regular, near daily, occurrence that entire school year. Flaming Hot Cheeto, anyone?

Deodorant Girl

Many students feel uncertain and self-conscious in the locker room, especially in their first middle school year, packed in like sardines, toe-to-toe, and dressing in front of their peers. However, a few students arrive on the scene full of confidence. Deodorant Girl carried herself with this aura of self-assurance. She became well known for her unabashed and extreme style of deodorant application. While everyone was grateful for her regular application of deodorant, they were constantly amazed at her confidence in style. She, as with many of her peers, did not yet wear a bra, but was unabashed when she would nearly disjoint her arm by putting it behind her head, to slather on layers of deodorant, patiently coating one armpit after the other.

Belly Button Weekend

A teacher was in the Physical Education office one morning when the bell rang for the students to go outside for class. One wide-eyed teenage girl approached the teacher, arm extended, with a rumpled note in hand. The teacher reminded the student to put on her uniform and head outside for class, but the girl hesitated. She told the teacher she would not be suiting up because she could not participate. The student did not appear sick and had no obvious injury, cast, or brace. Perplexed, the teacher asked the student why she could not participate. The student replied, smirking, that her belly button piercing was infected. Thinking she had not heard the student correctly, the teacher asked the student to clarify. The student once again told the teacher that her belly button piercing was *really, really* infected and that she couldn't participate. The teacher, not easily fooled, told the student that she did not think twelve and thirteen year olds could get a navel piercing. The girl lifted up her shirt, showing off a festering belly button piercing and joyfully told the teacher that teenagers can get a belly button piercing so long as their parent goes with them and says it's ok. She then proudly advised the teacher that she and her mom went together and got matching belly button piercings! The student then read aloud the note from her mom, which, indeed, verified it was a mother and daughter belly button piercing weekend.

New Pee Bag

Walking across the blacktop to meet his class, which was situated at their assigned student area, the teacher gave a friendly shout out to an exuberant, affable student. The kind of kid that brings joy to the classroom and all those around him. A laid back, surfer boy with a perpetual smile and easy-going nature. The teacher asked, "Joey, how's it going." He replied, "Its going ok." The teacher said, "It looks like you have a little limp to your walk?" Before the teacher could even blink, the happy-go-lucky kid pulled up his pants leg in front of the entire class to expose his pee bag while he blurted out, "I have a catheter! I won't be able to do P.E. for a while!"

Horse Back

11/15/16

To Mr ████████

Please excuse Riley from P.E. today. Riley was thrown from her horse yesterday and landed on her back.

Thank you for your time.
Mrs ████████ (Riley's mom)
████████

Skinny Jeans, Big Shoes…Not a Winning Combo

This is an amazing story of kids taking lazy to a new level. A kid came running up to the office in the Physical Education locker room to say that her friend needed help. The teacher, sensing a real emergency, ran to give support and help. When she arrived at the scene, she found a student who was stuck in her skinny jeans… couldn't get them up, couldn't get them down! The skinny jeans were stuck on the girl's shoes. The crowd of nearly 100 other students gathered round this genius time-saving girl to watch the nonsense unfold. With the crowd gathering, tension rising, and the student near distress, the teacher had to get the student to calm down. Together, the teacher and student were eventually able to remove the girl's shoes so the girl could then shimmy out of her doll-sized jeans. At this point, the teacher asked why she hadn't taken off her shoes before trying to remove her jeans. The girl replied in typical middle school tone, "UH, it takes too long to take off my shoes." It's moments like this when my two Master's degrees really come in handy. I could tell a version of this same story, different kid, at least a dozen times. This lazy business is becoming an epidemic.

Self-Imposed Confinement

One student again approached the P.E. teacher for immediate help with another student, and, recognizing the panic in her tone of voice, the teacher ran to the aid of the student. This time, the kid was stuck in her own locker. Yep, her very own P.E. locker. The same place where stinky running shoes and sweaty uniforms live. For reasons known only to middle school students, this kid thought it would be fun to be inside her foul 10-inch by 30-inch metal locker. To her delight, she managed to squeeze herself in. Then, she panicked and began hyperventilating. Imagine trying to calm a panic-stricken adolescent as she struggles to free herself from her own self-imposed confinement, all the while surrounded by a hundred giggling teenage onlookers.

Nailed for Stabbing

Dear Jacob;

    I am sorry for stabbing you with my nail. It was not nice and I am sorry. ~~The~~ I will controll my anger next time and not hurt others around me.

    I was angry because I did not get my way. Instead of ~~a~~ pushing you I will just grab another jump-rope. I am very sorry and I will controll my anger and just go tell ███. ███████ if I have a problem.

          From: Sima ████████

Just When You Think You've Heard it All…

A teacher was standing in front of her class taking attendance as the bulk of the students stretched. During this time, a male student named Singh hobbled over to his female teacher with an excuse note. The note stated the student was unable to do Physical Education for a few days. The student announced quite boldly that he had his foreskin removed. While the teacher tried to catch her breath, the student asked, "Do you know what a foreskin is?"

Stash Pocket

A sincere student apologetically reported one day to his teacher that he would not be able to wear his Physical Education shorts for a few days. The teacher inquired why not, as this was an earnest young man who strived to attain the highest marks and took the P.E. apparel very seriously. The student stated that he had VERY important keys that he must keep with him at all times. Since his Physical Education shorts had no pocket to accommodate his keys, his shorts were at the tailor for a pocket to be sewn in so that he could keep the keys safe and on his person. BTW: This kid who no doubt grew up to become a successful young man is likely now a Silicon Valley superstar.

Treats for Everyone

So, here I am the newbie teacher at the middle school with Principal Fattest Man Ever. I had been told by fellow teachers and the office secretary that the principal LOVED to bring in treats for his teachers and staff. Wow, what a nice guy, I thought to myself. In fact, he did LOVE to bring in treats. On a regular basis, Principal Fattest Man would be seen waddling through the office with not one, but two big pink boxes full of donuts, pastries, and other sweet treats. One for the staff lounge and one for his desk. Indeed, the Fattest Man would consume the entire big pink box of treats from the comfort of his oversized office chair. How do I know? I popped in to say thank you every time he brought treats, and there he sat gobbling down the goodies.

Classroom Observation

About half way through the school year, Principal Fattest Man let me know that he would be observing me in my classroom and then making his recommendation about me as a teacher. I had been expecting this, as I knew it was part of the normal first-year procedures. Arrangements were made about which class (math or P.E.) would be observed and during which period. Ultimately, it was decided that he would observe one of my P.E. classes during a basketball unit. So, being proactive, I stopped by Principal Fattest Man's office the day before the observation to confirm the final plans. I happily reminded him that he would be observing my afternoon P.E. class out on the blacktop during the basketball unit. Principal Fattest Man said, "No, no, no, no, no, no," wagging his finger back and forth. He then explained that he would not go out to the blacktop. In fact, he would not leave his office. Instead, he told me that I would bring my entire classroom of students up to the front office, where they would do their lesson outside his office, and he would crack his door open and observe from the comfort of his oversized desk chair. How one performs a basketball unit without a basketball court was beyond my comprehension, but realizing that Principal Fattest Man was not walking out to the blacktop, I had to change my plans. The next day, my entire class performed a jump rope exercise outside the office door, while Principal Fattest Man sat back in his comfy desk chair and briefly observed. He gave me a glowing review.

He/She

Shocking Parent Comment

Teachers are often called upon to participate in high-profile student meetings involving the student's parent. During these meetings, teachers and others share their professional observations and insight about a student. One such meeting, which included at least a dozen well educated pro-student individuals, was held on behalf of a middle school student. Many of the people present shared their professional perspective on the individual student, all with reports filled with data and statistical information about the student's progress. The meeting moved at glacial pace as each professional enlightened the group from his or her individual perspective. The group was tasked with making best decisions for the student. People grew weary as the meeting dragged on when, much to the surprise of everyone in the room, the student's mom said she understood and she blurted out about her own child, "Sometimes retard, sometimes not!" Meeting adjourned.

Knee, Dog, Skates, etc.

MISS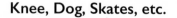

PLEASE EXCUSE DANIELLE
FROM P.E. TODAY.
SHE FELL AND SCRAPED
HER KNEES YESTERDAY
WHEN A DOG CHASED
HER WHILE RIDING HER
ROLLER SKATES.

THANKS

IF YOU HAVE ANY QUESTIONS
CALL ME ON MY CELL

Dear ████████████ 12·9·08

Joshua ████████ was messing around last night and smacked his ankle on a fire hydrant. It is bruised and swollen. Please excuse him from P.E. for the next couple of days.

Thank you—

Jen████████

"Sock Surprise"

One day a kid was hobbling around campus and I asked if he was ok. He said he
hurt his foot. I asked if he needed a Band-Aid and he said he just needed to sit
down and might use a Band-Aid. He took his shoe off, but was hesitant to remove
his sock. I said, "Hey if you hurt yourself, let me get you an antibacterial wipe and
a Band-Aid." He pulled off his sock, and to my surprise, revealed bright blue toe
nails freshly painted. I could see why he was hesitant to take off the sock.

IBS

PZ

Jan. 29, 2011

It's constantly something, I know. For the past week [redacted] I.B.S. and reflux has been playing. He has an appt. in two weeks with his G.I. doctor. His I.B.S. (irritable bowel syndrom) is causing him a lot of pain, and jumping, bouncing, skipping, running etc. are not ok for him right now. He may walk and be more stationary. I will get a doctor's note if needed, please let [redacted] know if you need that.

Also, please put him to work somehow so he has a purpose out there, both for his sake and his grade sake.

Thank you,
Brandi

P.S. call if you need to:
[redacted] my cell

Starter Pistol

This story happened long before school shootings were an issue. There was an ongoing problem with an older gentleman who came onto the schoolyard while school was in session. He would show up regularly as if he were headed to the golf course, carrying his golf bag, wearing the golf gear, and carrying a bucket of practice golf balls. Numerous times teachers asked him to please wait until school was over to hit the golf balls. He just kept coming back. One day one teacher had enough, went inside, got the track and field starter pistol, and walked out with starter pistol in hand. Students scattered and screamed as the startled golfer took off and was never seen again.

Why Locker Rooms Need Air Conditioning

During the beginning of the period on a particularly hot day, students were getting changed into their Physical Education clothes. A teacher was at her computer when she heard a very nervous voice say, "Hey teacher, teacher!" When the teacher turned to look at the student, she saw a girl who had her hand up by her ear and a look of complete fear on her face. The teacher realized the student had a hand-held fan that had gobbled up her goldilocks. Major fan surgery took place in the locker room. While performing fan surgery on poor Goldilocks, the other 100-plus kids in the locker room displayed an experiment in inverse proportion: their patience got less and less while the heat grew more and more.

Rough Play Sunday

Meet Me at the Bike Rack

Another Open House gone awry. Mom, dad, and kid walked up to the teacher as if it is their own private prescheduled meeting. The teacher thought it's a friendly meet and greet, but much to the embarrassment of the kid and perhaps the mom, the dad in a loud voice said, "We're going to settle this right now!" The teacher, a bit taken back, asked, "What are we going to settle right now?" The teacher thought back to her middle school days and those words usually meant a fight at the bike racks after school. In the end, the dad was upset that his kid, who is a "Serious Softballer," wasn't getting a free A in Physical Education. As dad continued with his monologue tongue lashing, the teacher maintained a straight face. Another teacher nearby, sensing trouble, quickly asked the entangled teacher for help with some amorphous task. Never happier to be asked to help with such banality, the teacher excused herself without laughing out loud.

Cheers

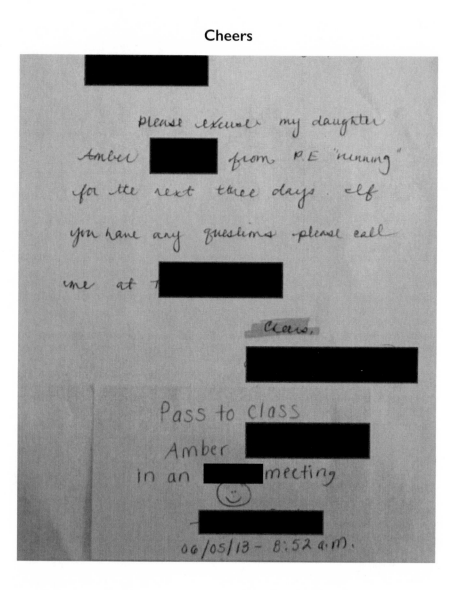

Please excuse my daughter Amber ▮ from P.E "running" for the next three days. If you have any questions please call me at ▮

Cheers,

▮

Pass to class
Amber ▮
in an ▮ meeting

06/05/13 - 8:52 a.m.

Principal Darkside

Set the scene: The principal was walking side-by-side with the P.E. teacher, taking in the scenery of hundreds of middle school kids as they ran around and played nearby. The principal leaned in to the teacher and said, "I am so glad I'm not a teacher anymore, I just can't stand the kids!" Fade out.

Helicopter Parents

"I think that instead of helicoptering our kids, we should be strapping some parachutes on their backs made out of things like common sense, kindness, and courage. Then we should teach them to jump."

JOELLE WISLER

AYSO Semester Off

Fat Mom in Her Own Words

Enrique called from school and said he was sick so I had someone pick him up because I work in Long Beach. While he has had a sore throat the past two days, I didn't think he was sick enough to stay home. I could sense that something was wrong. Turns out he is not sick enough to come home, he's humiliated and sitting home alone crying about a stupid PE mile run. Seems there is some question as to whether or not he cheated to get the time of 7:53 and that you don't understand it because he runs the cross in over 9 minutes.

Here's what I would like to do. I am going to personally bring the boy to school or you can do it, whichever you prefer. He is going to re run the mile. If he doesn't get close, I will deal with that and he will deal with the consequences and apologize to the kids and you for cheating. If he does make it, I feel like you should apologize because the other kids are obviously clued into the fact that you think he cheated because a couple of them, ⬛ Sharp and another kid whose name I forgot (maybe Grant) stated that "Even Ms. ⬛ thinks you cheated".

If my kid is getting hassled so bad at PE that he can't even get through the day, something is wrong because this kid is not a baby in any way. You may consider the following. You specifically said on his report card that he needs improvement and I discussed that with him. Any possibility that the two miles he's walking my dog every day are helping? Any chance he actually tried? Another fun fact is that he has just finished a 30 day physical fitness requirement for Boy Scouts where he had to log his improvements in sit ups, push ups and mile walk/jog. Further, he recently did a 9 mile backpack hike with 35 pounds on his back. He doesn't like running so he doesn't try very hard at the cross. That does not make him incapable of running a mile in 7:53.

I am a fat mom and I promise you, noone is more interested in him not turning out like me than I am. Here's another thing I know for certain. It's completely wrong to belittle him, doubt him and help him get teased by not handling your doubt with him alone rather than in front of others. Doesn't middle school suck enough

already without any help from your teachers making you feel bad? This is not encouragement which is what I would expect.

Let me know your thoughts on rerunning the mile.

Follow Up with Fat Mom

In response to the tone of Fat Mom's email, the teacher felt it best to call her on the phone to diffuse the situation and to reach an amiable solution. During the call, Fat Mom made it clear her "boy" would prove he ran the mile in 7:53 and she would bring him to campus after school to be timed while the teacher watched. Knowing the student consistently ran the cross (3/4 mile) in over 9 minutes, the teacher had no doubt he could not run the mile in 7:53 and she felt sick to her stomach at the certain outcome for fear the student would have hurt feelings. But, Fat Mom had made a mountain out of a mole hill and she was determined to put the teacher in her place and secure an apology for her boy. The student and his mother arrived on campus after school to meet the teacher for a pre-scheduled re-run of the mile. The mother insisted the teacher apologize to her boy after he proved his running prowess and, to appease the mother, the teacher agreed that if the student ran the mile in 7:53 or less, then she would, indeed, apologize to him. To make sure there was no question about timekeeping, the teacher gave mom the stopwatch. They then reviewed the course to make sure the student and the mom knew where to run. After confirming the student knew the course and his mom could successfully operate the stopwatch, the one boy race began. As the student slowly and laboriously cantered along the course, his mother was intently focused on the stopwatch. As the minutes ticked by and the student inched along, his mother's face took on a look of defeat and abject horror. In contrast, the teacher's agony was mounting as she watched the student's struggle increase. The teacher experienced no joy as the truth was revealed. When he finally completed the mile (somewhere north of 12 minutes) red faced and panting, Fat Mom accepted the fact that her boy had not been entirely dedicated to the truth in reporting his earlier run time. Needless to say, the apology came from the student to the teacher, who gently thanked him. Fat Mom then slinked away with wounded pride.

Big Breakfast

Dear ▮▮▮▮ Office 9/22
Staff;

Please switch my
son, Jonah ▮▮▮▮
from 4th period to
5th period lunch.
because he eats
a big breakfast
and isn't hungry
during 4th.

Thanks so much,

Big Game Tonight

6/8/09

Mr. ████████

Please excuse ████████ ████████
from P.E. today as he has
an important Baseball game tonight

*Please - don't have him dress out, but
and use the time to - do homework

Thank you.

Rebecca ████████████████

Respect My Decision

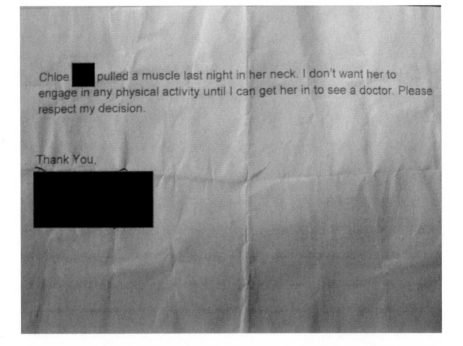

Chloe ▮ pulled a muscle last night in her neck. I don't want her to engage in any physical activity until I can get her in to see a doctor. Please respect my decision.

Thank You,

Competitive Cheer > PE

I wanted to follow up with you about grading for PE. I know we spoke after the quarter grades came out and I had asked you about extra credit as well as what they were going to be graded on for the upcoming quarters in PE. You mentioned extra cross runs as the extra credit option. ████ tried to come a few times, but I believe she was only able to do one run. You had mentioned that they were going to be graded on doing push ups this quarter also and I wanted to make sure she did okay on that.

I had a chat with another 6th grade parent today who is in Mr ████ class for PE. She mentioned that her child was able to receive extra credit throughout the quarter for extra workout type things done outside of school and signed off by the parent. She told me that her child was receiving a low score in PE due to slow run times and that this extra credit has brought her child's grade up to an A.

I was under the impression from our conversation about statewide standards, expectations and grades that all the PE teachers were grading on the same standards. With this conversation in mind, I think it is imperative to let you know that ████ is on a competitive cheer team that practices twice a week for 2 1/2-3 hours each practice. She has been on this team without interruption since before school started. During practices they stretch, run, jump, do push ups, sit ups, lunges, etc. as well as work on tumbling/gymnastics, dance and build partner stunts. It is a very aerobic and demanding sport and I would be happy to bring you dvds of her performances as well as documentation from her coaches. I am hoping that this can be used as extra credit for her grades for 1st semester as well as for the upcoming semester.

I have no intention of being a problem parent, I am just trying to be an advocate for my daughter. Please let me know your thoughts on this matter.

Thank you.

Sunshine Fresh Laundry

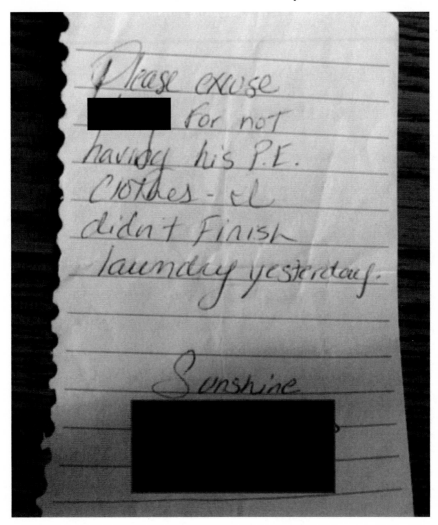

Soccer > PE

March 4, 2010

████████████████

Physical Education Department

To Whom it May Concern,

Please excuse my son Taylor ████ from strenuous physical activity in P.E. class today. He has been experiencing groin and quadricep pain and would like to rest it in anticipation of playing soccer for the school team later today.

Regards,

████████████████

Dance Competition > PE

Please excuse [redacted] from running the cross today as she is in training for a dance competition [redacted]

Taylor

Sock Police

Every few years, a parent treats an Open House like a personal parent conference vendetta opportunity. On one such ruinous night, a parent approached a physical education teacher and wagged his finger in the teacher's face while talking wildly. The parent lectured the teacher at great length that she was "not the sock police" and that, although hygiene is an issue, it is not the teacher's job to comment if a student is or is not wearing socks. The real irony in the teacher's mind was that just a few years prior it was the norm to tell families that their children were not only required to wear socks, but they were specifically required to wear white socks during P.E. class. [Hello – it is not obvious that sweaty feet in athletic shoes fare better when encased in comfortable white cotton socks...]

Speed Kills

Please excuse Chad ████ from running the cross today, he hurt his leg at Speed Kills last night

Beth ████

3/25/10

Serenity No Taunting Pledge

Don't laugh at me
Don't call me names
Don't get your pleasure from my pain
Can't you see we're all the same

The No-Taunting Pledge

I will pledge to be part of the solution

I will eliminate taunting from my own behavior

I will encourage others to do the same

I will do my part to make my community a safe place by being more sensitive to others

I will set the example of a caring individual

I will eliminate profanity towards others from my language

I will not let my words or actions hurt others

AND if others won't become part of the solution, I **WILL**

Student commitment Serenity ███████

Parent Acknowledgement _____ X _see attached memo_

Date ███████

Why We Defy the Pledge

I understand the monumental task of keeping students safe at school in an increasingly hostile society filled with angry children. I have always supported efforts such as your "No Taunting Pledge" in the past, and I regret to inform you that I cannot support this pledge, as it has been written and implemented. More importantly, I cannot expect my children to sign the pledge as written.

This is a moral, ethical, and legal dispute of the text used in the pledge and of the heavy-handed method of implementing and enforcing compliance. Simply stated, I will not force my children to sign anything that contains the following:

- Eliminate profanity and taunting behavior (sentences 2 and 6)

- Assume responsibility for the solution and exempt "others" from same (sentence 8)

- Required to sign with pen to permit punishment for violating pledge (teacher instruction)

- Compliance gained through threat of grade reduction by one letter grade (teacher instruction)

You may think these are benign points, perhaps even trivial. However, my children are being coerced into signing, in pen, a document that your staff intends to enforce as if it were a binding contract. The items I list above are wrong for the reasons below:

- My daughters have no profanity or taunting behavior to eliminate, so signing this pledge would be an untrue admission of guilt and no guarantee of good behavior.

- When "others" do not resolve the problem, my 11-year old daughters are not responsible for taking up the slack. Sentence 8 merely exempts the problem children while holding accountable the children who are not the problem.

- Requiring children to sign this document in pen to ensure compliance is wrong and misguided, no contract signed by an individual under the age of 18 constitutes a binding agreement. For this reason, I have not signed this pledge to protect my children who naively signed the document during school today.

- My children work very hard on their academics. Discipline is an administrative concern and simple non-compliance with a faulty document does not warrant an academic penalty. I trust that you will not punish my children because I decided to return the pledge documents without my signature.

Be assured that my children have indomitable morals, which mandate the very values your pledge attempts to regulate into practice. Civic duty, equity, justice, honor, and compassion are the values by which my two ██████ students live. Moreover, these are the very characteristics that prevent and can eliminate taunting and bullying. My husband and I spoke long and earnestly with our children and they understand that we are not being defiant or rebellious by not signing the pledge documents. We simply are protecting our daughters against any further encroachment.

Thank you,

████████████████████████

Fever Stay Home

12/12/1

To whom it may Concern,
Grace ███████ WAS sick
on Friday with a high fever.
In the future, I've asked her
to be more persistant when
she feels ill in order to
protect her health.

Thank you,

███████████████████

MD Says Student Can Decide

Address _____ City _____

NOTE: Authorization for refills other than marked will only be given Monday - Friday from 9:00 - 5:00

Rx above patient is able to perform physical education a only as tolerated

Refill Authorized 0 1 2 3 times _____ M.D.

Prescriptions must have watermark to be valid

49

Foot Blister Epidemic

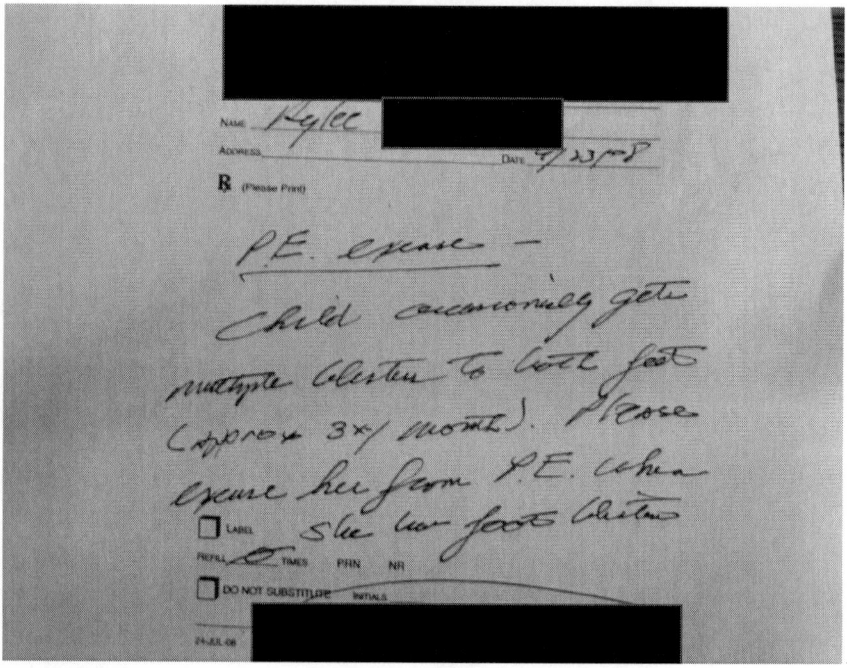

Sprained Weist?

To whom it may concern: ████ ████ sprained his weist so he can not do anything with it.

Ted ████ 1/27/2009

Can't Suit Up

Weds. 10/13/10

Please excuse Kaitlyn ▮▮▮ from
suiting up for PE. She has a
pretty bad cough that gets worse when
she runs.
Feel free to call me if you need to
confirm.

2-Day Hypothyroid Problem

Stomach + "Allery" = Legs

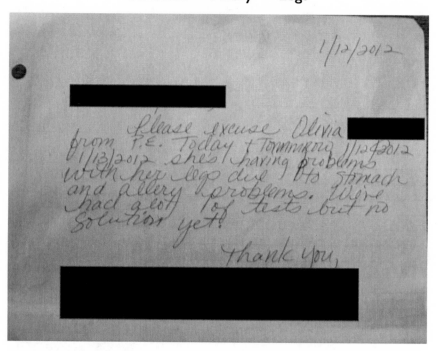

Domestic Duties Struggle

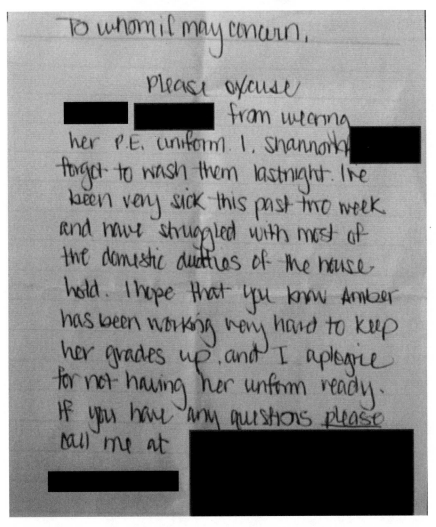

To whom it may concern,

Please excuse ██████ ██████ from wearing her P.E. uniform. I, Shannon ████ forget to wash them lastnight. I've been very sick this past two week and have struggled with most of the domestic duthes of the house hold. I hope that you know Amber has been working very hard to keep her grades up, and I aplogice for not having her unform ready. If you have any questions please call me at ██████████

To whom it may concern
Sunshine has expressed concern
regarding another student regarding
her weight. Could Sunshine please
have the school nurse record her
weight?

If there are any concerns
please contact me a)

"Teacher Ogre"

A student's parents requested a teacher conference, but to the school staff member's surprise, they wanted to meet not only with the teacher but also with the administration. The student was a decent kid with no academic problems and no behavioral issues. The reason for the meeting was unclear. The teacher and the administrator spoke briefly beforehand. Neither one was sure why the parents wanted the meeting and, more curiously, why they wanted them both to attend. The mystery meeting took place in the Assistant Principal's office and the parents seemed agitated from the beginning. The Assistant Principal, being a thoughtful and detailed person, assured the parents that everyone had the same goal in mind, which was to help their child be successful in school. During the conference, the parents asked typical questions about classroom procedures, grading, etc. They did not ask any questions that suggested there was a problem to address. Deep into the conference, the parents finally began to simmer down. After what seemed like a benign (and thoroughly unnecessary) parent conference, the parents stood up and shook hands with everyone. They then announced quite proudly that the teacher wasn't nearly the ogre they expected based on their child's description.

Excessively Excessive

Dear Mr █████████████   6-1-07
                                         ⌖⌖⌖

    Please excuse Amanda from running the cross. Last time she ran it 100% (vs running part way & walking the rest of the way) she ended up with a severe headache & muscle aches because this distance is excessive for her. She needs to take smaller jaunts to work up to it. Having PE 1st period, the headache & muscle affected her in the rest of her classes for the rest of the day & into the evening here at home. Therefore I am going to have to ask that she not be pushed this excessively in running it 100% of the time █████████████

American-Made Pencils

At a parent teacher conference, two brothers and their mom and dad sat with a teacher. The teacher went over grades, homework, and how both boys often were unprepared and unwilling to take notes in class. The dad quickly turned to his sons and became visibly upset about them not using their "American made, top quality pencils" that he bought them for school. About 20 minutes later, the dad was still proudly talking about these American made pencils. The conference lasted nearly 90 minutes with nothing accomplished except a lengthy paternal monologue about the overwhelming success of the American made pencil. [Clearly, he missed the "point" of the meeting!]

Student Shams

I'm always disappointed when a liar's
pants don't actually catch on fire.

"Heart Burns"

Rachel has been having heart burns so she can't do P.E

Multiple Choice Excuses

Dear Ms. ███████

Please excuse Sarah from
running because:
a. Her knee hurts
b. Her ankle hurts
c. Her stomach hurts
        Thanks,

Locker Devil

Lesson Learned?

Dear Ms. ██████████

I hope you learned ur lesson
Sorry about the black ripped shirt.
Maybe you will consider this
next time. Do not interfere
with my right to use my
own locker. ⊘ We did nothing
but help you learn your lesson

P.S. If you havent
realized where your clothes
are... look towards the sky.
Sincerely,
the wind

65

Missing Shorts = Locker Room Hideout

Mrs ████████ -
. you marked
Nick ████████ absent
for 2nd per. Mom
says his shorts are
missing & wondered
if he was hiding in
locker room?? Please let
me know if you saw
him later. Thx
Jolene

Fake Domestic Duties Struggle

THREW OUT HER LEG

Please excuse Katie from PE. She threw out her leg during ballet and can't run. Thank you

Who has the "Cuncution?"

Trouble All Around

Dear Mrs. ██████████ 10 12 10
please excuse Katie ████████ from
doing P.E. she has a bad cough
and can't run she has trouble
breathing. Thanks,
    Debi ██████████

        ████████████████

Cough

        asthma?

Straight into a Hole

Mrs. ▇▇▇▇▇,

Gabby's ankle really hurts. She sprained it at soccer the other day. Her foot went straight into a hole. She is unable to run today.

LISA

ON HER PERIOD.

"Sincereley" not Well

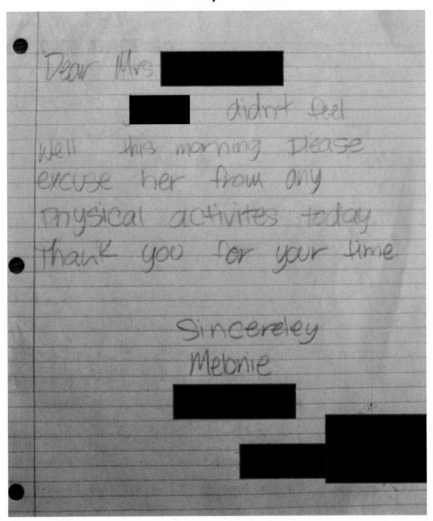

Dear Mrs ▮▮▮▮▮
▮▮▮▮ didn't feel
Well this morning please
excuse her from any
physical activites today
Thank you for your time.

Sincereley
Melonie

"Right" Another Note

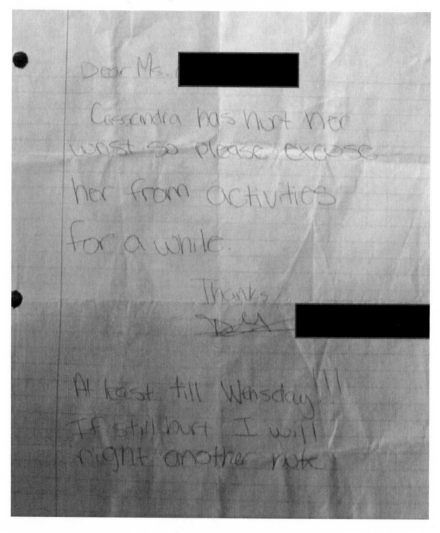

Fudged Date

Simpsonisms

I will not cut corners.
I will not cut corners.
I will not cut corners.
I will not cut corners.
I will not cut corners.
I will not cut corners.
"   "   "   "   "
"   "   "   "   "

BART SIMPSON
JANUARY 24, 1991
"ONE FISH, TWO FISH, BLOWFISH, BLUE FISH"

F-Word

I will not say the f-word.
I will not say the f-word.
I will not say the f-word.
I will not say the f-word.
I will not say the f-word.
I will not say the f-word.
I will not say the f-word.
I will not say the f-word.
I will not say the f-word.
I will not say the f-word.
I will not say the f-word.
I will not say the f-word.
I will not say the f-word.
I will not say the f-word.
I will not say the f-word.
I will not say the f-word.
I will not say the f-word.
I will not say the f-word.
I will not say the f-word.
I will not say the f-word.
I will not say the f-word.
I will not say the f-word.
I will not say the f-word.
I will not say the f-word.
I will not say the f-word.
I will not say the f-word.
I will not say the f-word.
I will not say the f-word.
I will not say the f-word.
I will not say the f-word.

Suck It

X _____

1. I would not yell out "suck it" in class when 5th graders are touring
2. I would not yell out "suck it" in class when 5th graders are touring
3. I would not yell out "suck it" in class when 5th graders are touring
4. I would not yell out "suck it" in class when 5th graders are touring
5. I would not yell out "suck it" in class when 5th graders are touring
6. I would not yell out "suck it" in class when 5th graders are touring
7. I would not yell out "suck it" in class when 5th graders are touring
8. I would not yell out "suck it" in class when 5th graders are touring
9. I would not yell out "suck it" in class when 5th graders are touring
10. I would not yell out "suck it" in class when 5th graders are touring
11. I would not yell out "suck it" in class when 5th graders are touring
12. I would not yell out "suck it" in class when 5th graders are touring
13. I would not yell out "suck it" in class when 5th graders are touring
14. I would not yell out "suck it" in class when 5th graders are touring
15. I would not yell out "suck it" in class when 5th graders are touring
16. I would not yell out "suck it" in class when 5th graders are touring
17. I would not yell out "suck it" in class when 5th graders are touring
18. I would not yell out "suck it" in class when 5th graders are touring
19. I would not yell out "suck it" in class when 5th graders are touring
20. I would not yell out "suck it" in class when 5th graders are touring
21. I would not yell out "suck it" in class when 5th graders are touring
22. I would not yell out "suck it" in class when 5th graders are touring
23. I would not yell out "suck it" in class when 5th graders are touring
24. I would not yell out "suck it" in class when 5th graders are touring
25. I would not yell out "suck it" in class when 5th graders are touring
26. I would not yell out "suck it" in class when 5th graders are touring
27. I would not yell out "suck it" in class when 5th graders are touring
28. I would not yell out "suck it" in class when 5th graders are touring
29. I would not yell out "suck it" in class when 5th graders are touring
30. I would not yell out "suck it" in class when 5th graders are touring
31. I would not yell out "suck it" in class when 5th graders are touring
32. I would not yell out "suck it" in class when 5th graders are touring

Not Act "Iniproprietly"

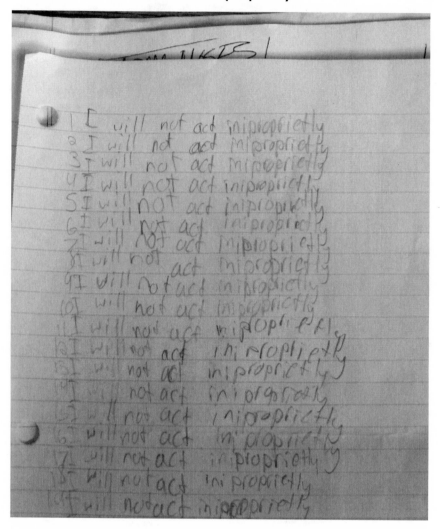

Ditching is Bad

JUSTIN

Ditching is bad because you can get hurt and no one well be there to help you, some one kun kidnap and the school is responcebal for you and If you or hurt or serting the school well ne in trouble.

Ditching is bad because You can get hurt and no one well be there to help you and I could make moters worse and the school can get sewed and lose a lot of money.

another reson ditching is bad is some one could kidnap you and you might nevir be scen agin and think you on flace the school can got sewed and lose a lot of money.

No Gum Nick

1. I will not give Nick gum before school.
2. I will not give Nick gum before school.
3. I will not give Nick gum before school.
4. I will not give Nick gum before school.
5. I will not give Nick gum before school.
6. I will not give Nick gum before school.
7. I will not give Nick gum before school.
8. I will not give Nick gum before school.
9. I will not give Nick gum before school.
10. I will not give Nick gum before school.

Seriously, It will not happen again!
Randy ████

It's All in the Name

"Could you just call me Pigeon? He asked the teacher
when she read his name. Does your mother call you
Pigeon? No. Then to me you are Paul….. Nathan Sutter,
the teacher read. My mother never calls me Nathan. "Is it
Nate?" the teacher asked. No, she calls me Honey Lips."

BRANDON MULL, THE CANDY SHOP WAR

Harry Dong

During the opening of another school year, a student teacher sat alongside the veteran teachers at a table, helping write students' names on Physical Education uniforms. The procedure was: the student would write his or her name on a 3x5 card, hand it to the teacher with his or her uniform, and wait while the teacher used terrific penmanship to write each student's name. Startling the crowd, the 6-foot 5-inch student teacher leaped to his feet and told the kid, "Don't mess with me just because I am new here. Tell me your real name." A veteran teacher looked over, saw the name on the card, and tried to settle the dust for Harry Dong, and told the student teacher, "That is actually his real name."

Harry Dong Part 2

During the afternoon meeting between a 6-foot 5-inch student teacher and a mentor teacher, the recap of the day led to a conversation about a story that occurred the previous year. A teacher had called home to ask the parents if there was a nickname for their son Harry, as his name made it difficult for him in Middle School. The parents said, "No. This is the name we chose for our boy." "We named him Harry and you will call him Harry"...sorry Harry Dong.

Miss Dick

A middle school female student needed her name written on her Physical Education shirt. This particular year, the protocol was that it was the teachers responsibility to make sure all names were spelled correctly and written neatly. The student requested that the teacher write her nickname and not her full first name. The teacher then asked, "What is your nickname," and she said, "Cat." The teacher said, "Nope. Not doing it." The kid said, "That's not fair." The teacher again claimed, "We won't refer to you as 'Cat Dick' this year."

Vikings Vick

Over time, the Parent Teacher Student Association (PTSA) took over writing names on the Physical Education apparel (previously known as uniforms). One year they came up with a terrific idea to save all the man hours used with people writing on the shirts: the PTSA developed a form. This form showed a sample shirt and written in perfect penmanship, "Vikings, Vick." The PTSA believed each child's guardian would write his or her child's name (Last, First). When veteran teachers got wind of this idea, they told the PTSA it might not fly. The PTSA said not to worry. Sure enough, the first week of school, there were many students who reported to campus wearing their Vikings, Vick apparel!

That's My Real Name

A new student teacher was assigned to observe and teach at our middle school. His name was Matt. He was asked to teach a lesson to the class, and before the students arrived, he wrote his name on the board. Known to be a humorous person and willing to kid with the middle school students, he wrote "Mr. Wiener" on the board. We said Matt, we don't think that's appropriate for middle school kids. He seemed a bit embarrassed as he probably has many times in his life and said, "That's my real name! But I will have them call me Mr. Why-neer."

Master Herpes

Students were out on the field doing a cardio day (the dreading running day), as one student ran past the teachers and said that he was getting made fun of by another student who was calling him fat. The teachers called the student over who was accused of being mean. The student whose name was Herpes responded, "I wasn't being mean." He defended himself by saying, "All I really said was chubb chubb, chubb, chubb," while moving his arms like a train locomotive. The teacher asked, "Is there any way that you can understand that this would hurt the other students feelings?" The student named Herpes replied as if he had no idea, and the teacher replied using a different approach. "With a name like Herpes, has anyone ever made a comment about your name that made you feel badly?" THAT hit a nerve.

Ribald

Referring to sexual matters in an
amusingly rude or irreverent way.

That Gesture

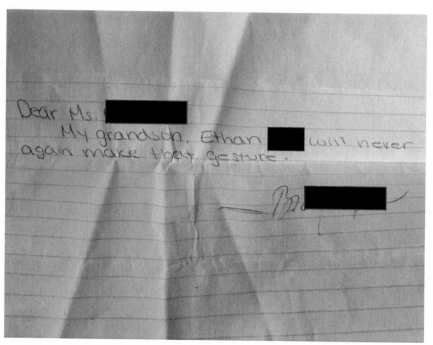

Until I Squeal!

During a relatively quiet time of instruction to approximately 90 6th graders, a teacher heard an unusual sound. She stepped around the group of kids to where a student was sitting off to the side, rubbing a quite private area of her body. The teacher politely asked the student to please be quiet during instruction. The student, who was wearing ear phones (causing a lack of vocal volume control) blurted out for all to hear, "I do it until I SSQQQUUUUUEEEEEEEAAAAAAALLL!" The teachable moment for the class quickly changed direction.

Adolescent Cootie Catcher

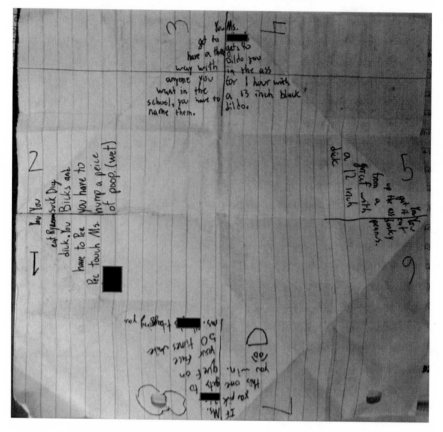

"Hookups"

I was in my office at about 8 a.m. Two 8th grade girls knocked at the door and asked for my help. One was speaking for the other, as middle school girls often do, and asked if I could take a look at the back of her throat to see if there was anything wrong. Faced with this odd request, I asked why? The girl, speaking for her friend, said she had a long weekend and hung out with "a lot of high school guys." I asked, "What does that mean?" She said she "hooked up" with multiple guys and suspected she might have "gotten something" from one of them. My teacher training kicked in as I peered into her throat using a phone as my flashlight. I saw what appeared to be bumps in her mouth and throat, so I recommended visiting Planned Parenthood during her off time. Sure enough, one week later, I got the news: the girl's friend and spokesperson told me her friend had strep – the bumps were not from the crazy hookups.

PEN15 Club Part 1

During a track and field unit in Physical Education, a teacher was going over the proper handling of a baton during a relay race. As the teacher described the concepts of the passing lane, acceleration, and teamwork, the teacher noticed an adolescent male student in the back of the class who appeared to be disengaged. While the teacher tried to remain focused on the lesson, he noticed the young male student sitting in the back of class was holding a baton and wearing a curious grin on his face. In the blink of an eye, the teacher quickly realized the overjoyed kid was handling the baton like he was home alone in his bedroom... with the door shut tight.

PEN15 Club Part 2

As a new teacher at school, I often looked to my mentor teacher for ideas and for tips on how he led his Physical Education class. I eagerly sought ideas for classroom management and curriculum insights. One particular day, I noticed his class sitting in a group observing a soccer drill. A lone boy stood in the back, using one of the soccer cones as his makeshift oversized penis, just swaying it back and forth. To my astonishment, without saying a word, my mentor teacher walked right over to penis boy and head butted him to the ground. I ran over and asked my mentor what he was thinking. He simply said, "Watch my class. I am heading to the office to report my inappropriate behavior." My mind was racing: would he lose his job, would his teaching credential be revoked, etc. Needless to say, this was a stressful day which led to a sleepless night. The next morning, my mentor teacher walked right up to the principal's office anticipating a meeting with the boy's parents. Nobody arrived; nobody called; where were they? The boy was called to the office and asked if he knew when his parents were coming. Penis boy said, "Are you kidding me? I didn't tell them about the teacher because then I would have to explain what I did."

Monkeyballs

name   time out   time in   Date
mrchen / 10:24 / 10:26 ⓑ
raylee   11:09   4:09
Daniel   ████   9:31
Jason
Tony   10:34
Daniel   9:54   9:57
nriel   9:57 – 10:00
kaylee   10:40   10:43   bathroom
Piper   10:43   bathroom
Trent   1:10   later
Austin   10:49   10:53 bathroom
F████ Reich
Ms. 16.████ sucks monkeyballs

Family Heirloom: "ROCK THESE"

A few years back when schools still had an expected dress code policy, a young lady appeared at my office door wearing what appeared to be a size 3T shirt that stated, "ROCK THESE," across the chest in bold black letters. I had a quick conversation about the distractability of the young men on our campus with her wearing that shirt. She responded with extreme shock and stated, "My Dad bought me that shirt!" I told her per school policy, she would need to change the shirt and her dad should come pick up the "ROCK THESE" t-shirt from me at his earliest convenience. She engaged in verbal warfare defending her ability to wear the shirt, due to the fact that her dad bought if for her and it was really important to them. Ten years later I still hold the "ROCK THESE" t-shirt heirloom.

Underwear to Work

The teacher walked into the locker room office to meet her new Physical Education colleague's sub for the day. There she was, sitting in her pink sports bra and short shorts, ready for a day at the beach, or so called sub day for middle school. The teacher, caught off guard, dashed up to the front office, found a very conservative administrator and said, "I am going to need your help with a situation." The administrator said, "Of course I will help you." The teacher sent the administrator to the locker room to tell the sub that she couldn't just wear her bra to work. The administrator, knowing the teacher had a dry sense of humor, thought this might be a joke, but she was game for a little fun. When she arrived in the girls locker room and realized, indeed, it was not a joke. There sat Suzy Sub in her bright pink sports bra ready for a day of Physical Education with middle schoolers!

A Really Good Read

As a teacher was walking through the hallway near the library, he peered into a classroom and noticed the students were taking a test as a substitute teacher, sitting up in a tall chair at the lab table, was deeply engrossed in a Playgirl magazine. (Back it up, read that again…yes, Playgirl magazine.) The teacher was taken aback, and hustled up to the office to report the situation to the administration. Later in the staff lounge, it was reported to the teacher that the sub wouldn't be coming back ever again. The administrator added that the sub claimed she was reading it only for the really good articles.

"Pants Down"

During school modernization, trailer-style portable bathrooms were parked on the school blacktop. During afternoon supervision one day, I had a strange sense that there was a problem near the portable bathroom. I thrust the door open, and much to my surprise the bathroom was dark, but the light from the doorway crept in and revealed two startled boys eyes wide. They struggled to explain why they were in the dark and near one another, also with their pants unkempt.

It Makes it Worth It

"In everybody's life at some time, our inner fire goes out. It is then burst into flame by an encounter with another human being. We should all be thankful for those people who rekindle the inner spirit."

ALBERT SCHWEITZER

Halloween #Legcramps

Dear Mr. ██████████ 11/6/08

   Carter was experiencing an unusual # of leg cramps last night. It is unknown if this is due to a sugar build-up from all that Halloween candy, or from an insufficient amt of nutrients not eating enough veggies... or from vitamins/nutrients being blocked from absorption... whatever the case... right now he's prone to the painful spasms & I am respectfully requesting Carter's abstinance from running today. He should be ok tomorrow to run (the cross) as we plan on flushing his system with plenty of water between now & then.

                REGARDS,

Really Bad Hang Nail

> 3-26-12
>
> Please excuse Chloe ▮▮▮
> from P.E. today. She
> has a really bad hang
> nail. I'm trying to get
> her into see a Dr after
> school. Thanks

Jacked Up Knee

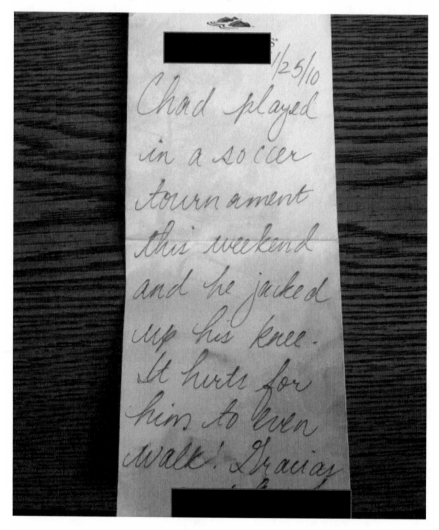

1/25/10

Chad played in a soccer tournament this weekend and he jacked up his knee. It hurts for him to even walk! Gracias

"Last Rights"

February 6, 2003

Savannah [REDACTED] has been lying
near death in our home for the
last three days. I was certain I
was going to need to call a Catholic
Priest to read her her "last rights".
She survived, so I made her go
to school on one condition — She
doesn't have to do PE on Thursday. ☺
All kidding aside — Savannah has a
Lung infection and is on antibiotics — She
cannot run today.

Sherry [REDACTED]

Middle Finger Problem

Dear Miss ▮▮▮▮▮▮▮▮▮

02/18/10

Susan has problem at her middle finger (on left hand)
She was played basket ball yesterday. Now her
finger is swollen. Could you excuse P.E for her
please!

I will take her to visit doctor tomorrow.

Thank you for your time to read my message.

Sincerely,
Susan's Father
TRily

Rousing Game

16 OCT 2008

Dear Ms. ████████,

Riley ███████ played a rousing game of flag football at the YMCA yesterday afternoon and as a result it looks like she strained her right hip flexor. Please excuse her from strenuous activity in P.E. today so as not to aggravate the strain.

Thank you,

Wonderbra

Borrowing vs Stealing

Layla

Dear Bailey,
    Sorry I borrowed your shirt and didn't give it back. It was not the right thing to do and I will never do it again, and Im also sorry for not atleast telling you I borrowed # it. Next time I will do the right thing, have my PE clothes and not use yours. I am very sorry for what I have done. I could have gotten you Im trouble. Your a great friend and I wish nothing would ever happy to you. I hope that we can get over my trouble and be friends but theres no excuses and ILL change my behavior Sometime I dont think before I do or say samthing. I will take your clothes without asking. Im sorry I even touched your clothes I will never take anything thats mine ever ever again

                your friend
                Layla

parent signature

parent signature
Layla is aware that this is stealing.

PE + Lunch Excuse

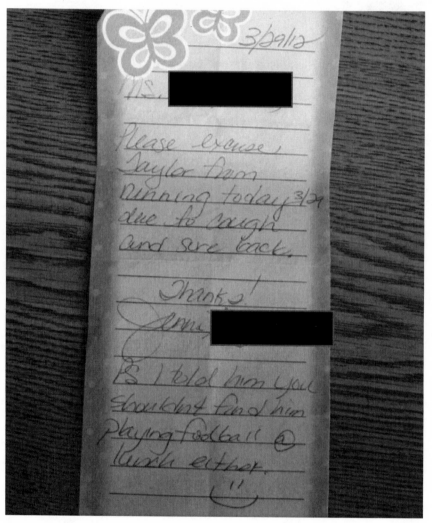

LEGS ONLY PE

Dear Miss ████████,

The doctor told us that Devin ████
could do P.E. for his legs after
4 weeks. It has been 5 weeks
and Devin would like to do PE
for his legs only.
Please include him in exercises
for his legs only.

Thank You
████████████
7/

Last Note of the Year

6-8-10

Dear Mr. ███████████

This will be my last note of the year! ha ha

Please excuse Allison from last Thursday until the end of the year — she is having many symptoms and is undergoing a variety of tests to see what's wrong.

If she feels ok she can participate.

Thanks,
Cynthia ███████████

Less Straight Forward

████████ let me know that you had thought I was mad in my email. I am sorry I was not mad at all. Sometimes emails come across in a way that does not come across the way they are meant. I am very direct and sometimes people think I am upset. I will try to be less straight forward and have more expression in my emails. I really was trying to figure out if grant really had a C and what he could do to bring his grade up. Thank you for your patience and I truly appreciate everything you do everyday and have great respect for all teachers as your job shapes a lot of how our kids grow. Sincerely Simone ████████

To Whom It May Concern: Sorry

To _____,

I am sorry for throwing the ball at you. I was frustrated because you and your friends kept putting me at the end of the line and I lost my temper. Im sorry for saying the "F" word. I won't lose my temper again.

Sincerly,

Trusted

M███████████

I just wanted to say thank
you for speaking up for Katie today.
I took her to the Dr right after school
and she is having muscle spasms in her
neck and has been in quite a bit of pain
It really meant a lot to both of us
that you trusted her today.
Thank you very much!   Debi ███████

Teacher Valentine

Dear Mrs. ████

You're a great P.E. teacher! I can now run 50x better! You really make sure that we aren't lazy and fat ☺. Besides that, you have a sense of humor, are very nice, very athletic, and I am very thankful to have a great teacher like you!

Happy Valentines Day,

Katie ████

Surprise Award

On an otherwise average day, to the surprise of teachers, the superintendent, assistant superintendent, and other administrators arrived at the school to alert a teacher nominee he would be winning the prestigious Teacher of the Year Award. Dressed in formal attire, this parade of administrators, carrying gifts, balloons, and signs, proudly walked through the halls out to the blacktop. On this day, for some unknown reason, the teacher nominee brought his puppy to school. He and his wife, the proud new parents of the puppy, chatted in the parking lot. His class was being supervised by other teachers, one of whom was involved in a competitive game of basketball with fellow students. Being alerted that the big wigs were on campus, the teacher ran back from the parking lot for his photo shoot with the congratulatory committee. Just weeks later, he was invited to bring his family to accept this award formally at the district office. After all the hoopla at the school site, the formal event was rather anticlimactic. The 20-year veteran teacher received his trophy, with his name misspelled, as his wife asked, "Is this it, or will you be getting a check with that trophy too?"

Locker Room Confidence American Pride

No matter the time, nowhere else in America do people stand still for the Pledge of Allegiance in their underwear. All across America, at the start of the school day, students are hustling to change into their Physical Education apparel. When the school announcement for the pledge begins, students stop in their tracks to pay respect. It is an amazing phenomenon that hundreds of students, all talking and bustling bodies of energy, just stop where they are, eyes transfixed on the flag. Once the pledge is complete, they then revert to high energy, high volume groups of youngsters and finish dressing as if there were never an interruption.

A Cool Apology

I am sorry I didnt dress out completely for P.E. I didnt dress out completeley because I thought if you didnt dress out you would be cool but, when I got the letter from school I realized that it was a stupid idea not to dress out. I was wondering what imidate steps i should take to imporve my overall class performance. I am sorry to waste your time by not dressing out completely for P.E.and sincerely hope that you will accpept my a pology. I will now try very hard to improve my grade in P.E and to dress out completely everyday until the end of the year.

Sincerely,

Christina

1,160%-1,170%

Dear M██████████

    I am sorry for being defiant and just flat out rude. I shall do my absolute best to dress out all the time and give 1,160% EVERY day! My mom wrote you a message in School loop. I will do whatever it takes to get an A+ and to get made up on the Pacer, and I will listen to you, following instructions, never chewing gum, and always, always, always giving 1,170%! Thank you.

       Sincerely,

          Sarah ██████████

Student Art Apology

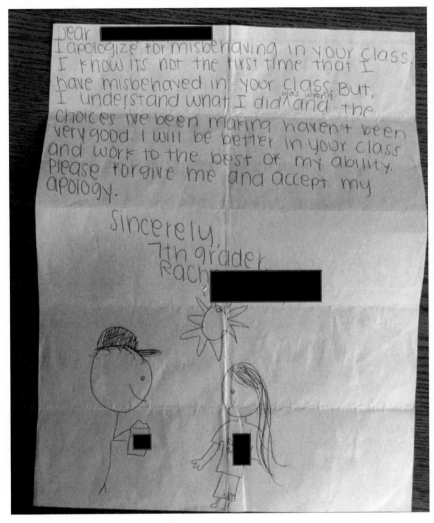

Dear ▮▮▮▮▮▮▮▮
I apologize for misbehaving in your class.
I know its not the first time that I
have misbehaved in your class. But,
I understand what I did ^was wrong and the
choices ive been making haven't been
very good. I will be better in your class
and work to the best of my ability.
Please forgive me and accept my
apology.

Sincerely,
7th grader,
Rach▮▮▮▮▮▮▮▮▮▮▮▮

Golden Rule

Dear ███████

respect means to me the golden rule. Wich is treat others the way that you would like to be treated. Also it means to clean up trash if you see it roll by you. To follow all the school rules also is very respect ful. Caring is also respect so if you care about your school then you respect your school. Finily respect is also politeness and manners.

From Trevor ███████

Proverbs Apology

Dear Ms. █████████

Sorry for what happen in tutorial yesterday I really mean it.

I really am a quiet person. I jostly get to crazy sometimes. Don't think of me as disrespectful or bad, please.

I've lost a lot of friends by being to loud.

There is a verse in the Bible in Proverbs that says:

"Watch your tounge and keep your mouth shut and you will stay out of trouble."
Proverbs 21:23

I guese I need to follow that more.

Again I am really sorry for what I did. I will be much quieter today.

Fondly,
Alex

Character "Edication"

12 words or more   Jake ▮▮▮▮

Character   Per #2

Character edication   relating

+10

Word bank:
- special Person
- love
- Caring
- affectionent
- Romance
- ~~the liftul~~
- thoughtfulness
- Kind
- respectful
- helpful
- apprecative
- forgiving
- sweet
- loyal
- unique

BUbble map on the
back ⟶

"Valitine" Art

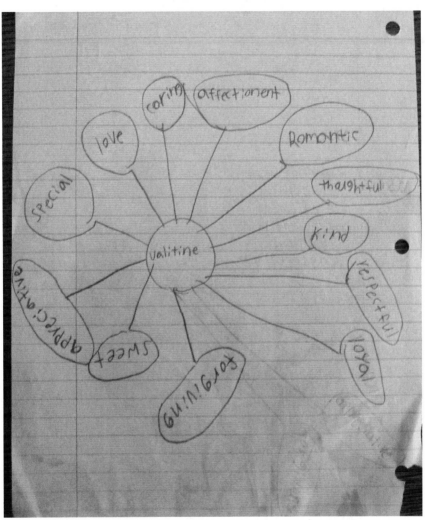

Heady Thanks

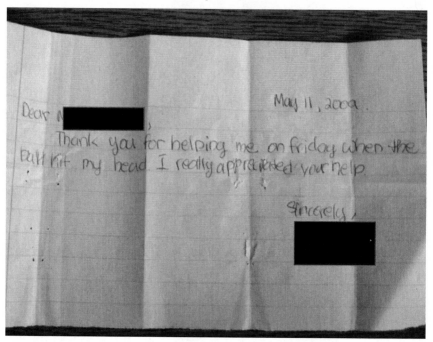

Dear N█████,   May 11, 2009.

Thank you for helping me on friday when the
ball hit my head. I really appreciated your help.

Sincerely,
█████

Forgery Note

Dear ████████████

I am very sorry for writing the note and forging the signature. I didn't mean to make excuses, but I really did throw out my leg, and my mom really did forget to write me one. But it was my decision to choose the worst option. I swear to you that I really was going to tell you the truth, but I was just too guilty to say the truth. Again, I am truly sorry and I hope that I can gain back your trust by forgiveness.

Your Student,

Note ████████████)

Acknowledgements

Parents and Kids - Many thanks for the overall goodness of kids and parents without whom this book would not exist.

DG 3 - Smartest guy in the room while seeing every shiny item that floats near.

DM - Thank you for making this project possible with your solid scaffolding and daily encouragement. I have deep gratitude for your unflagging support during this marathon project. You helped count the miles and keep my eye on the finish line.

H&H - Two supportive and giving people who have helped me grow into the man and husband I am today, forever grateful to the life you have provided me.

JI - Living proof that middle school students grow into amazing adults.

JS - Creative helper extraordinaire.

MK - To your incredible support and witty humor, your ideas and stories are truly what will make this the movie we always thought, thank you a million times for all you do.

Q - You were the first non-teacher to read our stories thoroughly and offer substantive feedback and encouragement. You are a gifted writer with a keen eye for detail, thank you for applying your skills to our project, turning rough stones into polished gems.

RS - One amazing human living a life planting trees under which he may never sit…thanks for teaching the enduring life skill of carpe diem since 1993.

SH - Thank you for your incredible energy and steadfast dedication to this seemingly ever illusive project. You never doubted we would finish and finish well. Your motivation has been a consistent fuel to the fire to finish this first of many collaborative projects.

TC 3 - Thank you for your recollection of a decade worth of amazing stories. As always you are a good scout, standing at the ready to make the film.

About the Authors

Mala Kral is a middle school educator with over 25 years of experience. Mala has a Master of Arts Degree in Teaching and a Master of Arts Degree in Theology both of which serve her well and daily in the trenches of middle school teaching. Mala is steeped in the live action study of adolescence and middle school culture. She sees her role as that of a seed planter, knowing adolescents eventually develop into civilized human beings. She counts herself blessed to have an amazing life – embracing the truth that not all who wander are lost.

Stephen Hawn is currently a real estate broker in Orange County who spent years in education in a variety of subjects, states, and grade levels. Stephen has a Doctorate Degree in Organizational Leadership and a Master of Science Degree in Educational Leadership. He is the Director of the Sport Management Program for Graduate Studies at California State University Long Beach and also serves as a Lecturer to mentor future teachers in Physical Education. Stephen also praises his time in the school system, having learned valuable lessons and skills and lives by the daily inspiration, "Education is what remains after one has forgotten what one has learned in school."

Contact the Authors

www.TheAppleDoesntFallFar.com

Follow us on Instagram: @theappledoesntfallfar

Like us on Facebook: facebook.com/theappledoesntfallfar